Air Marshal

and Careers in Transportation Security

Air Marshal
and Careers in Transportation Security
ISBN: 0-7660-2647-7

Border Patrol Agent
and Careers in Border Protection
ISBN: 0-7660-2646-9

Operations Officer
and Careers in the CIA
ISBN: 0-7660-2649-3

Search and Rescue Specialist
and Careers in FEMA
ISBN: 0-7660-2650-7

Secret Service Agent
and Careers in Federal Protection
ISBN: 0-7660-2651-5

Special Agent
and Careers in the FBI
ISBN: 0-7660-2648-5

Homeland Security and
Counter terrorism Careers

Air Marshal

and Careers in Transportation Security

by Janet Souter

Enslow Publishers, Inc.
40 Industrial Road
Box 398
Berkeley Heights, NJ 07922
USA
http://www.enslow.com

Library of Congress Cataloging-in-Publication Data

Souter, Janet, 1940–
    Air marshal and careers in transportation security / Janet Souter.
        p. cm. — (Homeland security and counterterrorism careers)
    Includes bibliographical references and index.
    ISBN 0-7660-2647-7
    1.   United States. Transportation Security Administration—Vocational guidance—Juvenile literature. 2.   Transportation—United States—Safety measures—Juvenile literature. 3.   Airports—Security measures—United States—Juvenile literature.   I. Title. II. Series.
    HE194.5.U6S69 2006
    363.28'7302373—dc22

                                                                        2006015849

Printed in the United States of America

10 9 8 7 6 5 4 3 2 1

To Our Readers:
We have done our best to make sure all Internet Addresses in this book were active and appropriate when we went to press. However, the author and the publisher have no control over and assume no liability for the material available on those Internet sites or on other Web sites they may link to. Any comments or suggestions can be sent by e-mail to comments@enslow.com or to the address on the back cover.

Photo Credits: Associated Press, AP, pp. 3, 26, 45, 50, 58, 67, 71, 73, 96, 102, 108; Corbis/Will & Deni McIntyre, p. 104; Federal Aviation Administration, pp. 5, 15, 17, 114–119; FEMA, pp. 18–19; Getty Images, pp. 6, 9, 33, 34–35, 57, 61, 65, 89; Getty Images/AFP, p. 14; Transportation Security Administration, pp. 5, 7, 8, 11, 22, 25, 28, 29, 30, 32, 38, 40–41, 43, 47, 49, 80, 81, 82, 87, 93, 105, 110, 126, 127, 128; U.S. Customs and Border Protection/Gerald L. Nino, pp. 5, 59, 77; U.S. Customs and Border Protection/James R. Tourtellotte, pp. 74–75, 120, 122, 124; U.S. Dept. of Defense, p. 37; U.S. Immigration and Customs Enforcement, pp. 95, 121, 123, 125.

Cover Photo: Associated Press, AP, Corbis/Royalty-Free (background)

The cover photograph shows a TSA instructor teaching a pilot how to disarm a potential hijacker during a class at the Federal Law Enforcement Training Center in New Jersey.

Contents

Chapter 1

Guarding the Skies

6

Chapter 2

September 11: A Wake-up Call

14

Chapter 3

Transportation Security Officers: Making Travel Safe

28

Chapter 4

TSA Technology: Staying Ahead of the Terrorists

58

Chapter 5

TSA-Trained Protectors: Bomb-Sniffing Dogs and Federal Air Marshals

80

Chapter 6

Planning for the Future

104

Chapter Notes   **114**

Glossary   **120**

Further Reading   **124**

Internet Addresses   **125**

Index   **126**

Transportation security officers check all bags being carried aboard airplanes.

Chapter 1

Guarding the Skies

The ten-year-old boy and his parents waited patiently in line at the security checkpoint at the Orlando, Florida, airport. They were tired and anxious to get on their plane to return home. Finally it was their turn to go through the security checkpoint. They placed their belongings on the conveyor belt to be x-rayed. The boy put on the belt a new teddy bear he had received a few days earlier.

The parents did not expect any problems, so they were surprised when the checkpoint officer stopped them. The officer had watched hundreds of items go through the X-ray machine that day, but something about the boy's teddy bear caught her eye. On the X-ray screen there appeared to be the outline of a handgun inside the toy. She stopped the boy and his family and took the teddy bear. Then the officer alerted the Orlando police and told them what she had seen. When the police officer examined the teddy bear, he found a half-inch hole in the bottom of the bear. He immediately tore open the bear and found a .22 caliber gun.

Federal Bureau of Investigation (FBI) officials questioned the family and were told that a girl at their hotel had given it to the young boy the day before. His mother had given her permission. The mother learned a valuable lesson: Never accept objects from strangers, no matter how harmless the object might appear. Fortunately, the family was allowed to continue their trip home.

The alertness of the TSA officer prevented a possible disaster. Her actions may have saved at least one life. If the boy had carried the teddy bear onto the plane, the gun

Even the most innocent-looking object can be used to smuggle dangerous items, such as a gun.

The American flag and the bald eagle—two symbols of freedom—are featured on the TSA patch worn by uniformed officers.

might have gone off accidentally. It could have killed him or other passengers.

A flight from New York City to Athens, Greece, started without incident. Then a passenger suddenly became violent. He refused to take his seat after several warnings from the flight attendants. The man threatened the pilot and attacked another passenger. Two men seated nearby had been quietly reading newspapers. When the commotion started, they sprang into action. They subdued the passenger and arrested him. The two men looked like ordinary passengers, but they were federal air marshals. Prior to the arrest, no one on board knew they were law enforcement officers except the captain and crew.

The pilot diverted the flight to Shannon, Ireland. There the air marshals turned the man over to the authorities. The flight continued to its destination.

These air marshals, as well as the transportation security officer who found the teddy bear, work for the Transportation Security Administration (TSA). It is a branch of the Department of Homeland Security.

The TSA was created after the terrorist attacks of September 11, 2001. People who work for the TSA are dedicated to fighting terrorism. They want to do everything possible to be sure Americans never have to suffer a tragedy like September 11 again. The people of the TSA know that terrorists threaten more than just air travel. Terrorists also target railroads, seaports, and mass-transit systems. Keeping Americans safe is an ongoing mission.

The TSA offers jobs like those just described and many others. All are challenging and demanding. Some jobs require a college education; others are offered to highly skilled people with a high-school education. This book describes some of them and tells you what you need to know to apply for a job with the TSA.

The TSA's Mission

According to the TSA Web site, the agency's mission is "to protect the nation's transportation systems by ensuring the freedom of movement for people and commerce."[1] The TSA works to make travel easier and safer not only for the American people, but also for businesses.

The TSA is the main agency controlling security at airports and during flights. It works to make sure

Besides air travel, the TSA protects other forms of transportation, such as national and local train systems.

seaports are safe for shipping and importing cargo. It is working to make rail travel and highways safer as well. It wants to be certain that people can travel safely on mass-transit systems such as buses and commuter trains. It is the TSA's job to stop mass-transit bombings, such as those that occurred in Madrid (2004) and London (2005).

The TSA is a division of the Department of Homeland Security (DHS). It works with U.S. Customs and Border Protection, Immigration and Customs Enforcement, the U.S. Coast Guard, and the FBI to handle emergencies and to prevent terrorist attacks. It also advises foreign airports of problems in their security operations. TSA employees use science and technology to prevent and handle threats to transportation security. The agency is looking at better ways to detect explosives and other dangers to passengers and cargo.

A Career with TSA

People interested in working for the TSA should think about their interests. Do you like helping people? When travelers go through the airport, they rely on TSA employees such as transportation security officers and security directors. Law enforcement agencies also depend on information from TSA employees.

For people interested in police work, there is the federal air marshal program. Federal air marshals keep passengers safe on airplanes. If a passenger threatens others during a flight, the air marshals keep that person from hurting others. All federal air marshals have experience as law enforcement officers.

For those interested in science or invention, the TSA is always looking for ways it can improve its technology. For example, it may be searching for a machine that gets people through the screening process more quickly. Other TSA employees are trying to find better ways to detect explosives. Many jobs at the TSA involve the law, administration, or teaching.

The TSA offers jobs for people interested in working with dogs that detect explosives. These people train dogs for law enforcement agencies or work as canine coordinators. A canine coordinator helps the dog handlers who work at airports, seaports, and railroad stations.

The Pentagon, the headquarters of the U.S. Department of Defense, was badly damaged in the September 11 terrorist attacks.

Chapter 2

September 11: A Wake-up Call

On September 11, 2001, people in New York City and Washington, D.C., woke up to a warm, late-summer day. They never thought that their lives—and the lives of all Americans—were about to be changed by tragic events.

At 8:46 A.M., American Airlines Flight 11 from Boston crashed into the North Tower of the World Trade Center in New York City and set the building on fire. At 9:03 A.M., United Airlines Flight 175, also out of Boston, crashed into the South Tower of the World Trade Center and exploded. Between 9:17 and 9:42 A.M., the Federal Aviation Administration (FAA)— the agency responsible for civil aviation, including air traffic control—shut down New York City airports.

The Port Authority of New York and New Jersey closed all bridges and tunnels in the New York City area.

At 9:43 A.M., American Airlines Flight 77 crashed into the Pentagon in Arlington, Virginia. By about 10:10 A.M., part of the building had collapsed. At the same time, United Airlines Flight 93 was hijacked. The passengers called friends and family on their cell phones

---

The passengers of United Airlines Flight 93 made a sacrifice so that other lives could be saved.

---

and the plane's airphones. They heard about what had happened to the other three flights. At that point, the passengers were fairly certain that the terrorists were planning to destroy the Capitol or the White House. It is uncertain what happened exactly, but flight recorders indicated that the passengers attempted to overtake the terrorists. Finally the flight crashed into a field in Pennsylvania. All people on board were killed. The passengers of Flight 93 made a sacrifice so that other lives could be saved.[1]

The FAA halted flights at all the nation's airports. Planes in flight were ordered to land at the nearest airport. International flights heading for the United States landed at Canadian airports or turned back to their airport of departure. It was several days before

On September 11, air traffic controllers helped land hundreds of airplanes that were in the air at the time of the terrorist attacks.

normal flight operations would resume. The U.S. military was put on high alert.

Creating the Transportation Security Administration

The hijackers on September 11 were able to take control of planes because they had weapons—box cutters, knives, and pepper spray. These weapons were not detected when the hijackers went through airport security. This mistake cost thousands of lives.

The TSA and Hurricane Katrina

The TSA's main role is to prevent terrorist attacks, but it helps Americans during other emergencies as well. In the summer of 2005, the TSA helped people after the devastation of Hurricane Katrina on the U.S. Gulf Coast. The TSA assisted in the evacuation of about twenty-two thousand hurricane victims from Louis Armstrong New Orleans Airport.[2] The DHS and the TSA sent 623 transportation security officers and federal air marshals to New Orleans from all over the country.

"Almost 20 percent of the passengers were in wheelchairs and elderly, injured or had special needs," said Michael Restovich, a federal security director who came from Texas to help.[3] "Our mission was to screen passengers—that's not what we did," Restovich says.[4] About four thousand of the evacuees had to be carried onto the 210 commercial and military medevac flights. Then the transportation security officers walked or carried passengers onto the tarmac and onto the planes.

Jon Holman, a screener from South Dakota, was one of 1,100 TSA employees who volunteered to help the hurricane victims. He lived in a hundred-person tent on the outskirts of Baton Rouge. Holman set up disaster-recovery centers and helped feed abandoned dogs and cats. He also sorted food donations.[5]

TSA workers still had screening to do as well. Security procedures were adapted to the situation. There was no electricity at the New Orleans

airport, so the transportation security officers had to pat down evacuees to look for dangerous items.[6] They took hundreds of weapons from the evacuees, but nobody was arrested. The transportation security officers understood that the people had knives and firearms for protection from criminals in the flooded city.

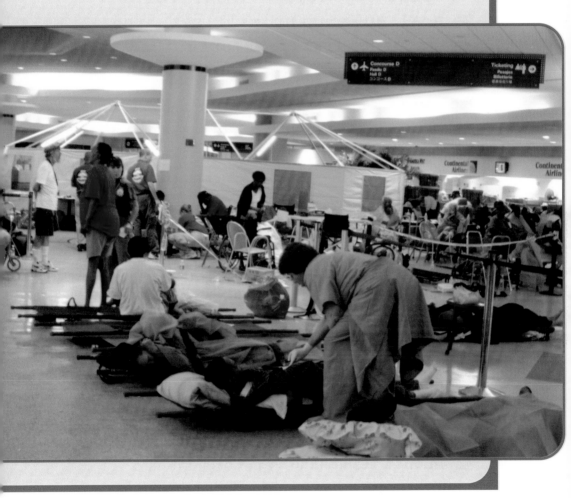

The federal government knew that it must work quickly to make airports and airplanes safer. On September 13, 2001, President George W. Bush vowed a victory over terrorism. One week later, he announced the creation of the DHS and appointed Pennsylvania governor Tom Ridge to head the department. The DHS

"Security comes first. The federal government will set high standards and will enforce them."

---

is responsible for making sure that all law enforcement agencies work together to prevent, to respond to, and to recover from terrorist attacks within the United States. It also handles large-scale emergencies such as natural disasters.

On November 19, President Bush signed the Aviation and Transportation Security Act. It established the Transportation Security Administration as part of the Department of Transportation. When the president signed the bill, he said,

> Security comes first. The federal government will set high standards and will enforce them. These have been difficult days for Americans who fly and for American aviation. A proud industry has been hit hard. But this nation has seen the dedication and

spirit of our pilots and flight crews, and the hundreds of thousands of hardworking people who keep America flying. We know they will endure.[7]

In March 2003, the TSA became part of the DHS. It joined several other government agencies that prevent and respond to catastrophes.

Building the TSA

Then the real work began. The new agency had thousands of jobs to fill. The biggest task involved hiring and training thirty thousand passenger screeners (now called transportation security officers). These are the people who work at airport security checkpoints. They check, or screen, passengers and their carry-on bags. They look for objects such as guns, knives, flammable liquids, and explosives. For more than thirty years, the airlines employed the people who checked travelers and their carry-on bags. However, these people were not trained well enough to detect all types of dangerous items. After September 11, members of TSA leadership decided that the transportation security officers must be highly trained to meet strict standards.

In January of 2002 the TSA had only thirteen employees. Congress gave it one year to hire, train, and place more than sixty thousand employees. By mid-2002 the TSA was hiring a thousand people per week to screen passengers and their luggage. Screeners

Along with examining carry-on luggage, security personnel check passengers' identification and tickets.

were hired for airports all over the United States, as well as the U.S. territories of Puerto Rico and Guam. By November 2002 the TSA had completed the hiring process. Security at the nation's airports was under the federal government's control.[8]

The TSA had four basic requirements for its security screeners. The screeners had to be U.S. citizens or nationals. They had to have a high-school diploma or the equivalent. They had to speak English well. Finally, they had to pass a background check and a screening for drug use. If they met these requirements, they were

---

Before the TSA took over airport security, screeners received only twelve hours of training. After that, they went through sixty more hours of on-the-job training.

---

tested on their ability to read X-ray images, to lift heavy objects, and to work well with all types of passengers.

The new employees had to complete forty hours of training. This included classroom and computer-based study. They were taught how to use high-tech screening equipment. Before the TSA took over airport security, screeners received only twelve hours of training. After that, they went through sixty more hours of on-the-job training with a more experienced screening supervisor.

November 19, 2001—The TSA is established as part of the Department of Transportation according to the Aviation and Transportation Security Act.

February 17, 2002—The TSA assumes responsibility for security at the nation's airports. Before that, the airlines were responsible for in-flight security and passenger screening.

November 19, 2002—The TSA meets the deadline for hiring its own federal passenger transportation security officers at airports across the country. More than 44,000 federal transportation security officers and 158 federal security directors are in place at 429 U.S. airports.

December 31, 2002—Every piece of checked and carry-on luggage is screened as of the required deadline.

March 1, 2003—The TSA is transferred to the Department of Homeland Security.

March 23, 2004—The TSA announces an agreement with the American Trucking Association (ATA) to expand the ATA's Highway Watch program. Truckers and other professional drivers learn how to spot and report security problems on the nation's roads.

June 2004—The Train and Rail Inspection Pilot (TRIP) is launched. This program would test new technologies and screening procedures at selected Amtrak and commuter rail stations.

July 2004— Registered Traveler Program testing begins at five airports around the country. The program uses fingerprints and eye scans to identify frequent travelers so they can get through the screening process more quickly.

October 21, 2004—The TSA works with the U.S. Coast Guard to begin using advanced explosives detection technology as part of the Secure Automobile Inspection Lanes (SAIL) test project. The program would conduct explosives screening on automobiles boarding the Cape May-Lewes Ferry in Cape May, New Jersey.

February 9, 2005—The TSA announces its Pledge to Travelers, a statement of rights and expectations for all people who go through the airport screening process.

August 18, 2005—The PortSTEP program is launched; homeland security testing for seaports begins.

September 28, 2005—National Explosives Detection Canine Teams are expanded to mass-transit operations.

December 2, 2005—The TSA increases training for airport transportation security officers, and officers are given more responsibility for the screening process.

At the end of 2005, the title of screener was changed to transportation security officer (TSO).

The TSA went on to establish tighter security measures at U.S. airports. By December 31, 2002,

A transportation security officer receives training on how to operate X-ray equipment to screen luggage.

> There are always ways
> to improve safety
> measures, and the TSA
> needs people to help
> them do just that.

the agency had installed 1,390 explosives detection systems. It also had installed 7,601 explosives trace detection systems at airport check-in areas where passengers board planes. These systems could find the tiniest speck of an explosive in any kind of container or on clothing.

The TSA still works to make travel safe and pleasant for airline travelers. Today private companies handle some screening, but all TSOs must be trained and cleared through the TSA.

The agency also knows how important it is to keep seaports, highways, mass transit, and trains safe. For example, it has TSOs working in railroad stations in some big cities on the East Coast. There are always ways to improve safety measures, and the TSA needs people to help them do just that.

A TSO greets a passenger at a security checkpoint. TSOs must be pleasant and professional while remaining vigilant about possible security threats.

Chapter 3

Transportation Security Officers: Making Travel Safe

More than 2 million air travelers and their luggage move through airports every day around the United States. Any one of those passengers could be carrying explosive devices in his or her checked baggage. Some travelers may have knives or other dangerous weapons in their carry-on luggage. Others may hide weapons in their clothing.

The vast majority of passengers are law-abiding citizens. They simply want to move through security checkpoints as quickly as possible to make their flights. The following story is an example of what a typical traveler might experience when flying on a commercial airline. We will call this traveler Mr. Smith.

What do TSA officers look for when inspecting a passenger's luggage? The list is long. Some objects seem harmless until they get in the hands of the wrong people. Here are some examples of items that are not allowed on any flight[1]:

- stun guns
- throwing stars (sharp, four-pointed, star-shaped weapons)
- dynamite
- fireworks
- flares
- hand grenades
- plastic explosives
- realistic replicas of explosives
- aerosol (except for personal care, such as hairspray)
- fuels (including cooking fuels and flammable liquid fuel)
- gasoline
- gas torches
- lighter fluid
- strike-anywhere matches
- turpentine and paint thinner
- chlorine for pools
- compressed gas cylinders (including fire extinguishers)
- spray paint
- tear gas

Before leaving the house, Mr. Smith checks the TSA Web site to get an idea of how long his wait might be at the security checkpoints at his departure airport. If he sees the lines are longer than usual, he may want to leave home a little earlier. That way he will not miss his flight.

Traffic is heavy on the way to the airport, and now Mr. Smith is running a little late. He arrives at the airport and goes to the check-in counter. Then he takes his luggage to the checked-bag screening area. The luggage is screened and taken to the airline to be loaded on the plane. Every step takes up a little more time.

As he rushes through the airport, Mr. Smith sees a law enforcement officer with a Labrador retriever. The dog sniffs an unattended suitcase. The dog finds nothing unusual about the bag. The law enforcement officer waits a few minutes to be sure the dog finds nothing and then moves on to make sure the suitcase gets cleared from the area. Mr. Smith arrives at the security checkpoint. A TSA worker asks to see his boarding pass and identification. She verifies that the documents are valid.

Mr. Smith places his carry-on bag and laptop computer on a conveyor belt, and they move under an X-ray machine. Like the passengers ahead of him, Mr. Smith quickly removes his shoes and places them on the conveyor belt. He also places his belt, watch, and coins in a special container so that they will not set off the alarm on the metal detector.

Concealed Weapons Show Up in the Strangest Places

Here are some of the concealed weapons TSA officers have found during security searches[2]:

- At Eppley Field in Omaha, Nebraska, a child's car seat was used to conceal a knife.

- At Luis Muñoz Marin International Airport in San Juan, Puerto Rico, a TSA officer found a statue concealing a sword.

- At the Minneapolis International Airport, the following concealed items have been taken at security checkpoints: brass knuckles, a grenade torch, a lighter shaped like a handgun, and a penknife.

It is a busy morning, and everyone is in a hurry. A person in a wheelchair needs extra attention from the transportation security officers. Mr. Smith waits as an officer carefully inspects the wheelchair. Then the officer helps the passenger go through the security portal. When the wheelchair passenger is safely on her

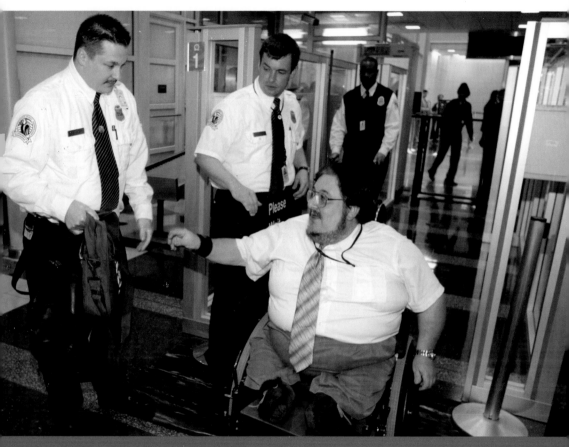

After being cleared by security, a man in a wheelchair leaves the checkpoint area. There are special screening procedures in place for people with disabilities.

way, Mr. Smith walks through the portal of a metal detector. The detector checks to see if he has any dangerous objects, such as a knife or explosives. He clears the final checkpoint. Then he gathers his belongings from the conveyor belt.

By now Mr. Smith is running late, but he knows the transportation security officers were just doing their job to keep everyone safe. He rushes to the gate and arrives in time to board the plane. There are many people on the flight. One of them could be a federal air marshal—another government employee who works to keep airplanes safe.

TSA Screeners at the Security Checkpoint

The helpful security employees who checked Mr. Smith are transportation security officers, or TSOs. TSOs, often referred to as screeners, have the official

Take Your
Computer OUT
of Its Case

IN
OUT
OFF

Transportation Security
Administration

Consumer Response Center, 1-866-289-9673

TSOs work around the clock, making air travel in the United States safe.

title of transportation security officer. They work for the TSA or for a company hired by TSA. They have been trained at a TSA facility. They want travelers to get through airport security as quickly as possible. At the same time, they want the travelers to have a safe and pleasant flight.

It is important to keep in mind that the TSA people are not law enforcement officers. The TSA supports law enforcement agencies and the airlines. For example, if a TSO finds explosive material, he or she must contact the airport's local law enforcement agency or the police.

People went through security checkpoints at U.S. airports before September 11, but now the screening process is stricter and more accurate.

These professionals take over from there. TSA workers know that cooperation with the other agencies is vital to keeping airports safe.

People went through security checkpoints at U.S. airports even before September 11. Most of the time it took only a few seconds. Now the screening process is stricter and more accurate. As in Mr. Smith's case, travelers may be asked to remove their shoes because some shoes have metal in them and could set off the

At San Diego International Airport in October 2005, a baggage officer found a suspicious object on a piece of carry-on luggage as it went through the X-ray machine. The object appeared to contain the parts for an improvised explosive device, or IED. An IED is a homemade object made of materials that become explosive when assembled. (Sometimes even normal items such as metal pipes can be used to make these devices, as shown in the example below.) The airport terminal was immediately evacuated, and bomb specialists investigated the scene.

When something like this happens, the owner of the luggage is stopped and taken for questioning. As it turned out, what the officer saw was not dangerous. Some passengers complained about the inconvenience the shutdown had caused. However, officers must take their jobs seriously. They have to make split-second decisions, always with passenger safety in mind.[3]

Many transportation security officers have gone above and beyond their regular duties to help people in difficult situations. On May 26, 2006, Lead Security Officer Richard Hale did much more. He saved a life.

Officer Hale was working at his checkpoint at Lambert International Airport in St. Louis when a couple came up to him and asked if he could call 911. They said a woman had collapsed nearby. Hale made sure someone could take over his post. Then he went to the woman. He found out she was diabetic. Fortunately, Hale also had military and medical training. He knew that she needed something that would help her brain signal her body to carry oxygen to all parts of her body, especially the lungs. Fruit juice would be best, but he had to get her conscious first.

Officer Hale raised the woman's feet to help her circulation and to encourage her to regain consciousness. He asked for a damp cloth for her forehead. Then, with some help, he turned her over on her side so she would not choke. An emergency medical team arrived, and the woman became conscious again and started talking. The airport's federal security director praised Hale for knowing how to handle the situation immediately and with confidence.[4]

alarm. The passenger then walks through the metal detector. If the alarm goes off, passengers must go through additional screening.

Some passengers may have a medical condition such as a weak heart. If he or she is nervous about being screened, the officer must make the traveler feel as comfortable as possible. The officer can write down instructions for people who are hard of hearing. If the passenger can read lips, the officer looks

TSOs can decide which travelers will need to be taken aside for more screening, even if they have successfully passed through security.

directly at the passenger while speaking. If a passenger has poor eyesight or is totally blind, the officer verbally explains the security process. The officer also helps the traveler put items on the X-ray belt and, if necessary, finds someone to help the traveler through the security process. People with prosthetic devices such as an artificial leg or arm must be screened with an explosives trace detection machine.

TSOs can decide which travelers will need to be taken aside for more screening, even if they have successfully passed through security. Officers do this randomly so that their choices will be unpredictable.

This is done so that terrorists cannot figure out how the officers make their decisions.

Many officers are trained to look for improvised explosive device (IED) parts. These items can include fuses, explosive chemicals, and power supplies to set off explosives. When they are put together, they become explosive and deadly. In other words, a passenger may have pieces of a bomb in his or her carry-on luggage, not a completely assembled bomb.[5]

At some airports, officers change security checkpoints every thirty minutes. This helps keep them alert and keeps their eyes fresh when they are looking at the X-ray machines. Sometimes the screens on these machines will display fake or "phantom" items that are not part of anyone's luggage. These are items that look like weapons but are not. They are designed to test the officer's ability to catch prohibited objects. Officers are

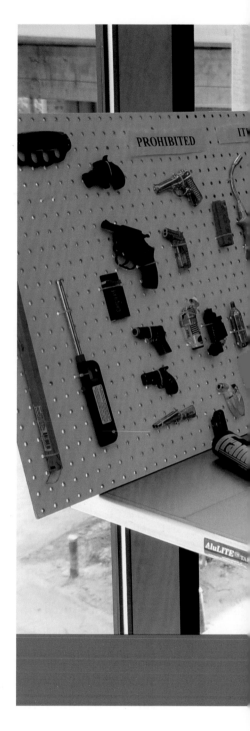

Knives, lighters, and even baseball bats are just some of the items that cannot be brought on an airplane.

retrained three hours each week to keep their skills up-to-date. They must be recertified every year.

Officers are trained to make pleasant conversation or small talk with travelers who seem suspicious. These travelers are usually looking around nervously or seem

---

Forbidden items include aerosol insecticides, cooking fuels, and fire extinguishers.

---

to be especially anxious as they go through security. During the conversation, the officer watches how the passenger reacts and speaks. TSOs are trained to know the difference between real threats and passengers who may just be running late for a flight.

Screening Checked Baggage

TSA officers also inspect checked baggage—baggage that will go in the airplane's cargo hold. An officer looks for baggage or cargo that may contain hazardous materials. Forbidden items include aerosol insecticides, liquid bleach, cooking fuels, and fire extinguishers. Baggage must be inspected quickly and accurately. If officers find a forbidden object in a passenger's baggage, they alert the airline and the airport authorities. They attempt to contact the traveler before the person boards his or her flight.

A TSO examines a bag for traces of explosives.

If a passenger's luggage contains a firearm such as a rifle or pistol, he or she must tell the officer or the person at the ticket counter. A TSA officer then inspects the luggage to be sure that the firearm is packaged in a hard-sided, locked container. The officer asks the passenger for the key in case the container needs to be opened for further inspection.

Sometimes the baggage is screened after the passenger has checked in. If the security workers see that the firearms are not packed correctly, they will contact the passenger. The passenger may have to repack the items. It may mean that the passenger will miss his or her plane and will have to arrange to take a later flight. However, it is better to upset one person's travel plans than to put a whole planeload of passengers in danger.

Baggage officers report to a lead officer. When the lead officer arrives for work, he or she makes sure there are enough officers to handle the workload. If there are not enough people, officers from other areas are sent over to the busy section. Next, the lead officer checks the machines to be sure they are working properly. He or she also obtains flight schedules to see if any flights have been canceled or delayed. There are baggage officers at large airports twenty-four hours a day. Some officers work from late afternoon to nearly midnight. Others come in late at night and leave early morning. Yet another group of officers work daytime hours from morning to late afternoon.

Air Marshal

An official from the Transportation Security Administration explains how the explosives detection system (EDS) works at the Dallas-Fort Worth International Airport.

ETD and EDS Machines

Many airports use the explosives detection system (EDS) and explosives trace detection (ETD) to search for items that are not allowed in checked baggage. Such items include flare guns, lighters, and gunpowder. If the TSA officer finds the items, the passenger may have to surrender them to local police. The TSA had these special screening machines in place by December 2002—about fourteen months after the September 11 attacks occurred.

An ETD machine is about the size of a large desk-top printer. To detect explosives, an officer runs a swab over a piece of luggage. Then the swab is

---

EDS machines are the
size of a minivan and
can scan several hundred
bags an hour.

---

analyzed for traces of explosives. ETD machines can find small amounts of explosive powders. However, it takes longer for them to detect hazardous material, so they are mainly used at small airports without a lot of traffic.

EDS machines are the size of a minivan. They work much faster than the ETD. They can scan several hundred bags an hour. Computers in the system look for objects with a certain density—that is, a certain thickness of material. Then they compare that data to the known density of explosives. Many everyday objects have the same density as these explosives, however. Thus, the EDS machine may set off false alarms. The officer must carefully hand-check the luggage each time an alarm sounds.

Federal Flight Deck Officer

In February 2003, Congress ordered the TSA to set up the Federal Flight Deck Officer program. This program allows flight crewmembers to use firearms to prevent a terrorist from taking control of the aircraft. The crewmember can be a pilot, flight engineer, or navigator. TSA employees teach crewmembers to use firearms and train them in laws, defense tactics, and other procedures. The training now includes pilots of cargo aircraft, such as people who fly for UPS or FedEx.[6] This is an all-volunteer program. Participants pay for their lodging and travel.

TSA employees must respect travelers' privacy as they go through the screening process. The agency has developed the Pledge to Travelers so that travelers will know what to expect when they travel.

Pledge to Travelers

- We pledge to do everything we can to ensure that your flight is secure.

- We pledge to treat you with courtesy, dignity and respect during the screening process.

- We pledge that if additional screening is required, we will communicate and explain each step of the additional screening process.

- We pledge to honor your request for a private screening at any time during the screening process.

- We pledge that if additional screening of your person is required, it will be provided by an officer of the same gender.

- We pledge to accept all feedback and to consider your input as a vital part of our effort to continually enhance the screening experience.

- We pledge to respond to your comments in a timely manner.[7]

The TSA Web site offers suggestions to passengers on how to dress, pack, and conduct themselves at the airport to save time during security check-in. There is a list of prohibited items for carry-on and checked luggage. A customer service center assists travelers with any concerns about the screening process. All these procedures are designed with the traveler's comfort and safety in mind.

To become a TSO, an applicant must meet several requirements, including having a high-school diploma or equal education.

Both ETD and EDS systems are effective. However, TSA engineers want to improve them so that there are fewer incorrect readings and they work more quickly. Sometimes the systems read an object as an explosive when it is not. Other times the systems fail to recognize an explosive.

Qualifications and Benefits for TSA Airport Staff

TSOs must have the following knowledge, skills, and abilities:

- the ability to understand, read, and speak English

- the ability to observe and identify various objects, shapes, and sizes

- knowledge of the screening process and its importance for the safety of the traveler

- the ability to operate screening equipment

- skills in communicating and working with travelers of various backgrounds

- the ability to lift baggage weighing at least seventy pounds

- good eyesight, hearing, and overall health

A person applying for a job as a TSO must meet the following requirements:

1. be a U.S. citizen or U.S. national

2. have a high-school diploma, general education diploma (GED), or equal education—or at least one year of full-time work experience in security, aviation, or X-ray technology

3. be willing to work odd hours, including evenings, weekends, and holidays

4. pass a drug and alcohol screening

5. pass a background check with no criminal record or poor credit record

6. successfully complete 56 to 72 hours of classroom training and 112 to 128 hours of training on the job

7. pass a final certification test

The salary for transportation security officers ranges from $23,600 to $35,400 per year. It varies depending on job performance, ability, and where the person lives. It is more expensive to live in some areas of the country than others. Keep in mind that TSA job opportunities are much more plentiful at major airports than at small, local airports.

The Road to TSA Airport Work

Many of the people who apply for work with the TSA work for private companies. Others have experience as law enforcement officers, in security technology, or working with machinery. Still others have been school principals, managers at large companies, or even airline pilots. They all have one thing in common: They want to do their part to be sure that an event like September 11 never happens again.

These employees accept the challenges—the unexpected incidents that happen every day on the job. As any TSA employee will explain, there is no ordinary day. "This is one of the challenges," said an officer who works at O'Hare International Airport in Chicago. "Passengers have lots of questions, which we try to resolve calmly. It's what I like most about the job."[8]

Numerous TSA support employees assist the TSOs as problems arise. For example, the screening manager helps them handle difficult passengers. He or she is available to answer questions about carry-on items or machinery that does not work properly. The lead TSO supervises the officers and screening managers. He or she makes certain that the workload is balanced and helps employees do their job better. A lead TSO or screening manager can earn from $30,000 to $40,000 per year.

If officers want to become a manager or supervisor, they have to take on more responsibility. Managers need

TSA Jobs at a Glance

Transportation security officer (TSO)	$23,600–$35,400
Lead TSO	$30,000–$40,000
Screening manager	$30,000–$40,000
Transportation security specialist	$36,400–$56,400
Federal air marshal	$36,000–$83,900
Information technology specialist	$36,400–$83,900
Contract specialist	$44,000–$83,000
Intelligence operations specialist	$44,000–$102,000
Canine coordinator	$54,000–$83,000
Engineer	$54,000–$83,900
Customer support and quality improvement manager	$66,000–$102,300
Federal security director (FSD)	$78,900–$157,200

skills for dealing with travelers. They must also deal with the people on their staff fairly. For example, screening managers must be certain that there are always enough workers at security checkpoints so that no employee becomes overworked.

The federal security director (FSD) is the person in charge of TSA operations at an airport. The director makes sure TSOs have what they need to do their job well. The FSD also makes sure there are enough people at each post. He or she places security staff members where they are most needed. The FSD also makes sure

> The federal security director is the person in charge of TSA operations at an airport.

the airport meets TSA security standards. He or she works with the local police officers and makes them aware of security risks at the airport.

FSDs also set up a system for crisis management. They must be able to work well with people on their staff. They are also responsible for setting up the security technology and maintaining it. These are only a few of the FSD's duties. The pay can range from $78,900 to $157,200 a year. The pay is high because the job has so many responsibilities.

Another TSA staff member at U.S. airports is the customer support and quality improvement manager. This person helps the FSD. He or she tries to prevent or to resolve traveler complaints. This person works with the FSD, passengers, airline staff, and airport retail stores. For example, if a passenger feels a TSO has mistreated him or her, the customer support person looks into the matter and tries to resolve it. This manager's salary ranges from $66,000 to $102,300 per year.

Stakeholder liaisons work with the FSD and the airlines to establish security policy. A stakeholder is an organization that operates at the airport, such as an airline, law enforcement officers, retail stores, and restaurants. These organizations have a stake, or interest, in airport security. A liaison is someone who acts as the middleman between two parties. If people connected with the airport have questions about security, the

Program analysts are troubleshooters—that is, people who solve small problems when they come up.

stakeholder liaison connects them with the TSA person who can best answer their questions.

Program analysts work as advisors to managers. They are troubleshooters—that is, people who solve small problems when they come up. They make sure equipment and employees are working well. If an employee is not doing his or her job according to TSA standards, the program analyst may suggest additional training. Program analysts also work to improve existing security systems.

Dangerous goods and cargo security inspectors determine how dangerous cargo should be transported and help with the inspection process. They need to know the laws about hazardous materials, and they help enforce those laws. People in this position need to be able to communicate with people who may not always agree with the regulations.

TSA employees help protect train stations as well as airports.

All the jobs within TSA airport operations are too numerous to mention here. However, all positions are in place to ensure the safety of the traveling public. Many of the jobs require a college education. All require patience in working with others.

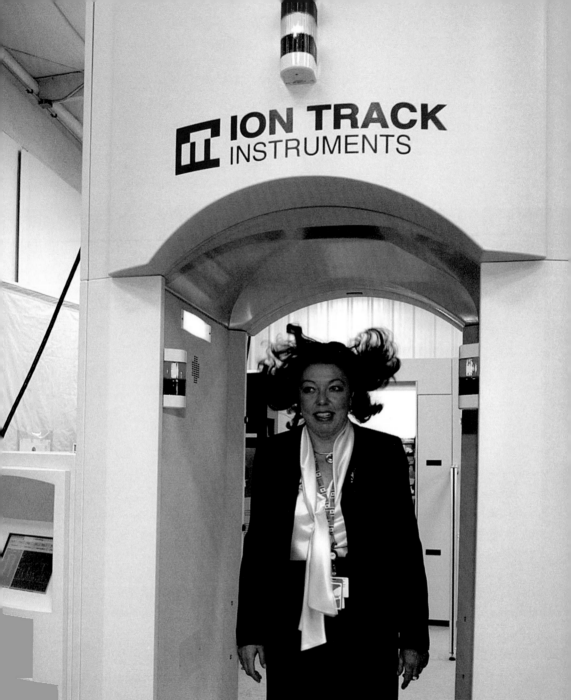

At the Transportation Security Laboratory in New Jersey, a staff member demonstrates a machine that searches for trace amounts of explosives on clothing.

Chapter 4

TSA Technology: Staying Ahead of the Terrorists

Both the TSA and the DHS offer careers for people interested in science, technology, and ideas. The TSA does research to make screening and explosives detection more accurate. Airports, rail yards, trucking facilities, seaports, and mass-transit operations all need this technology. Terrorists are working at improving their technology, too, so that explosive devices will be harder to detect. This ever-changing danger means that research and development (R&D) must go on.

When reading this chapter, keep in mind that some jobs are offered by the TSA and others by the DHS.

TSA Engineers

The TSA and the DHS partner with businesses and other government agencies to improve detection of weapons and explosives. Businesses make and improve these detecting machines. Then TSA engineers test them at airports, rail yards, seaports, and mass-transit facilities. These tests are called pilot programs.[1]

For example, if TSA engineers want to see how well an explosives-detecting system works in a rail yard, the agency will install it in a few different cities. If the

---

TSA engineers test detecting machines at airports, rail yards, seaports, and mass-transit facilities.

---

system works well, it can be tried elsewhere. These pilot programs are conducted for several months—maybe even a year—before they are offered to new places. The devices that work best are then put into operation.

The William J. Hughes Technical Center in Atlantic City, New Jersey, conducts R&D programs for the DHS. Sometimes TSA engineers who work with the R&D staff ask for a certain type of tool. They might ask for a system that can find explosives in a suitcase: "We need a system that can find an explosive that is this big. We need to know how fast it can screen a bag containing this explosive."[2] They might also decide how an explosive should look when it passes through the X-ray monitor. Perhaps it might appear a certain color on the screen, so that the officer can spot it.

They may ask for a device that works well under various temperatures in an airport or rail yard, for example. Engineers are always studying new technology and ideas that could benefit the TSA. They attend conferences, seminars, and meetings as representatives of the TSA.

A DHS or TSA engineer studies the equipment designs of many manufacturers and makes decisions about each one. They ask questions such as, "Will this

This device is called an explosives-detection document scanner. It checks a passenger's identification card and boarding pass for trace amounts of explosive material.

work?" or "Is it too expensive to produce?" Another engineer might ask, "If it costs this much to make, how much will it really increase passenger safety?" Someone else may suggest, "It takes too much time to operate." Then the engineers develop engineering standards, or rules. These include types of materials, part sizes, and

TSA engineers work with the people responsible for airport security to find out what they need.

how and where equipment should be tested. Then they ask what the new piece of equipment will cost. These and hundreds of other problems must be considered.

TSA engineers work with the people responsible for airport security to find out what they need. Then the engineers talk to the science and technology staff at the DHS to find out what is the most up-to-date technology available. Next, they write out what the security system has to do.

TSA engineers meet with the FSDs and the DHS science and technology people. It takes several meetings to work through the design. It must be of high quality, so the machines do not break down easily. Then the DHS finds a company to design the system. This company is called an outside contractor. It can take months for a system to be designed. Once a system is manufactured, it is tested at the DHS laboratory. When the testing team is satisfied that the system works, the TSA takes it to the appropriate facility to begin the pilot program.

People applying for a job as a TSA engineer must have a degree in one of several areas of engineering. These areas include mechanical, electrical, and industrial engineering, as well as other fields. TSA engineers may also need several years of related work experience. They must know physical science, computer science, math, and security technology. They must be able to speak and write about complicated technical information. Some may need a background in finance. A general engineer's salary starts at $54,000 per year and can reach $83,900 a year, depending on his or her education and years of experience in the field.

TSA Technologies

In addition to checked baggage screening discussed in Chapter 3, TSA engineers have helped to develop and test many new technologies. Some of these are now in use. Others are being tested in cities across the country.

Puffer Machines

As of 2006, TSA was using puffer machines to test clothing for traces of explosives in several airports around the country. At security checkpoints, passengers walk through a small doorway similar to a metal detector. Puffs of air are blown at them as they move through the doorway. The device then "sniffs" the air for traces of explosives. If any are detected, a traveler is stopped for questioning.

Document Scanner

At airports in several large cities, the TSA is testing an explosives-detection document scanner. The scanner swipes the surface of a document over a disc. The scanner tells the officer if explosive traces are on the document. If so, the passenger carrying the document is sent to another part of the airport for more screening.

Backscatter

The TSA laboratory is reviewing a technology known as the backscatter. This machine uses X rays to see inside objects. As passengers step into the machine, their image is outlined. This makes it easier for the officer to see prohibited items that may be hidden. Every passenger has the right to privacy, however. The TSA is carefully considering this issue, because it could mean that backscatter technology is not right for this use. The agency hopes to include software that will take care of privacy concerns. The backscatter will not be tested at airports until the privacy issues are worked out.[3]

Biometrics

Biometric technology is a system used to identify people by their unique physical characteristics. These

A TSA official shows how a document scanner can pick up traces of explosives on pieces of paper or plastic.

can include their fingerprints, their eye structure, the measurement of their hand, or the sound of their voice. No two people have the same fingerprint or retina (a part of the eye). If people change their name or carry false documents, their fingerprints or eye scan will help reveal their true identity. Fingerprint identification is the most common way to identify a person because the fingerprint almost never changes. Only in rare cases, such as an accident or burn, do

> If people change their name or carry false documents, their fingerprints or eye scan will help reveal their true identity.

fingerprints change. Identifying people by the image of their iris (another part of the eye) is becoming more common.

Biometric technology is used in the Registered Traveler Pilot Program.[4] In this program, frequent travelers volunteer to go through a security test. If they have no criminal history, they can be part of the program. Their fingerprints and eye images are recorded. When they travel, their fingerprints and eyes are checked as they go through the screening process. This shortens the time these passengers must spend at security checkpoints.

For people who fly frequently, the Registered Traveler Pilot Program allows them to pass through security more quickly.

The Registered Traveler Pilot Program was tested in 2005 at several airports around the country. When it becomes available for travelers around the country, private companies will operate it. People will pay a fee to be registered, but it is strictly voluntary. Travelers who are concerned with privacy will not be forced to use the program.

The program has some downsides. It is costly, and it could take another year or two to have it operating across

Rearranging Officers

High-tech inventions are not the only way to speed up the airport screening process. Sometimes low-tech solutions help, too. In a small room at the San Francisco International Airport, an employee watches several television monitors. He looks for long lines of people waiting at security checkpoints. If the employee sees a checkpoint where the line is especially long, he contacts supervisors. The supervisors send officers from slower areas to the crowded checkpoints. Sometimes officers are moved from place to place several times a day. This is one way the TSA can operate more efficiently.

the country. Program employees have to be certain that terrorists do not use false background information to join the Registered Traveler Program. Also, equipment used to read the people's fingerprints or retina images must be absolutely accurate. In early 2006 only the airports in San Jose, California, and Orlando, Florida, offer the program. There will likely be more in the years to come.

Biometrics is also used to screen people who apply for licenses to transport hazardous materials. Hazardous materials could be chemicals that explode or give off toxic fumes. These chemicals can be used to harm people. The TSA works with a private company on this program, which is known as the Hazmat Threat Assessment Program. The applicants submit their fingerprints and personal information. Then they go through a complete background check. Their fingerprints are sent to the FBI fingerprint database to be checked for criminal history. Once cleared, they are allowed to transport hazardous materials.[5]

The DHS and the TSA are currently working together with private companies to develop several improved security systems to fight terrorism. Some projects in the works as of 2005 included the following:

- A system that monitors a restricted area for outsiders. An example of this would be infrared beams that create an invisible electronic curtain around the area.

- A particle-imaging system that can detect explosives hidden in cars and trucks from a distance. The system provides a three-dimensional image of a closed vehicle and identifies the materials inside.

- Specialized equipment that protects firefighters from chemical and biological hazards.

TSA Pilot Programs: Safe Travel on Land and Sea

The TSA is working on making U.S. transportation systems more secure. The agency relies on information from the U.S. Coast Guard, U.S. Customs and Border Patrol, CIA, and FBI. It is important for government

The TSA welcomes suggestions from its employees on ways to speed up the security screening process. Pamela Friedmann is a program developer for TSA. She found a way to help frequent travelers move through the airport more quickly and with fewer hassles.

After September 11, Friedmann decided she wanted to play a part in the war on terrorism and accepted a position with the TSA. Friedmann believed biometrics might help fight terrorism. She developed the Registered Traveler Pilot Program with this technology in mind. About ten thousand passengers volunteered to test the program. Once accepted to the program, their fingerprints were recorded and their irises photographed.

From then on, whenever they arrived at the airport, they checked in at a special security kiosk. Their fingerprints and iris images were scanned and matched to the recorded data. Once their identity was confirmed, the passengers went to the head of the security line. They passed through the metal detector and ran their carry-on luggage through the X-ray machine.

The program participants were never selected for a random search. This helped them pass through security checks more quickly than travelers who were not prescreened. Friedmann feels that when law-abiding travelers can skip the screening process, it is that much easier to detect dangerous passengers. Officers can focus on fewer travelers at a time.[6]

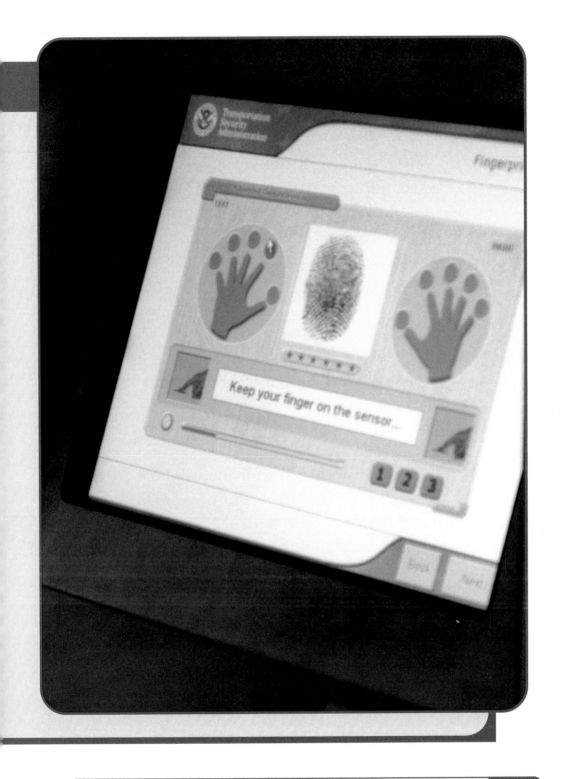

TSA Technology: Staying Ahead
of the Terrorists

agencies to cooperate with each other. This helps ensure travelers' security. The TSA depends on its staff members to come up with ideas to achieve this goal.

In 2004, terrorists bombed a railway station in Madrid, Spain. More than 1,500 people were injured, and 191 people were killed. In 2005, four bombs exploded on London subways and on a bus. Fifty-two people were killed, and seven hundred were injured. These bombings made Americans even more aware that terrorism could affect them at any time and in any place.

Today test programs in several railroad stations in the eastern United States check for hidden explosive devices inside passengers' baggage. Local agencies are responsible for security measures on buses, subways, and other forms of mass transit. The TSA works with them to plan and improve security. It also works with transportation operators to develop tools and computer software. These tools identify security weaknesses and help create better security plans. Many projects around the country are in the pilot phase. Below is a brief sampling of some of them.

PortSTEP

The TSA and the U.S. Coast Guard have created the Port Security Training Exercises Program (PortSTEP). It is a pilot program to make ports more secure. PortSTEP managers will work with other port security operations that are already in place. Employees at ports will be trained to handle a suspicious cargo container or an explosion at a seaport rail yard. The TSA and the Coast Guard will test how well security people communicate with each other at forty seaports. They will watch how they work together in emergencies. All this helps to determine how port security personnel react to possible or real dangers.[7]

This intercity train was destroyed in the 2004 terrorist attack in Madrid.

The TRIP Program

How is the TSA making rail travel safer for passengers? The Transit and Rail Inspection Pilot (TRIP) is the DHS's first study of rail security. TRIP was piloted in three phases at rail stations in major U.S. cities. Phase I occurred at a Maryland rail station. It studied the use of technologies for screening rail passengers before they boarded a train. Phase II took place in Washington, D.C. It tested the use of screening equipment for checked baggage and cargo before they were loaded onto an Amtrak passenger train. It also tested screening of unclaimed baggage and items stored inside the station. Phase III occurred onboard a rail car. It checked technologies that screened passengers and their baggage for explosives while the car was traveling.[8]

Operation Safe Commerce

The TSA's Operation Safe Commerce pilot project is a system to track cargo. It tests electronic seals that are attached to trailers or shipping containers. The device acts as a safety lock to keep the container from being opened or disturbed. It also tracks the shipment's location using the Global Positioning System. This is a series of communication satellites that can find the location of a point on the earth's surface. Next, the seal checks the

Working with the U.S. Coast Guard, the TSA has a special program designed to improve security in America's ports.

temperature of the cargo. This tells when a truck or container moves or its doors have been opened without permission.[9]

Highway Watch

The TSA helped expand a program called Highway Watch, operated by the American Trucking Association. Highway Watch trains drivers of commercial vehicles to report possible safety threats on the nation's roads. Truck and bus drivers, highway crews, tunnel toll collectors, and others will learn how to avoid becoming a target for terrorists. They will also be trained to spot and report suspicious activity.[10]

Careers Behind the Scenes at the TSA

The TSA's exciting technology and pilot programs have one thing in common: TSA staff members—along with colleagues at other government agencies and private companies—helped to develop them. There are many opportunities for people who want to come up with new ideas to make U.S. travel safer. There are also positions for people who want to turn those ideas into reality.

The public usually sees TSA employees at airport checkpoints. However, the agency offers many behind-the-scene jobs as well. These staff members contribute a great deal to the agency's mission. Here is a brief sample of TSA career opportunities.

The TSA has been studying ways to make train travel safer.

Transportation Security Specialist

Transportation security specialists inspect airports and air carriers to be sure their security systems meet TSA standards. They test security systems and write about their findings. Some TSA security specialists recently inspected the airport in Bali, Indonesia. They found several problems with the airport's security system. The

TSA could not reveal the problems, but they worked with the airport to make it more secure.

Transportation security specialists must be college graduates. They must also complete a four-week course

---

A contract specialist must have some education in accounting, business, law, or economics.

---

on security inspection. Transportation security specialists earn from $36,400 to $56,400 per year. Their salary depends on the area where they live, their education, and their experience.

Contract Specialist

A contract specialist is another TSA staff member. People in this position work with companies that have contracts with the DHS. These companies design and manufacture security products or technology. They may also provide TSA-trained officers and screening services at some airports.

The contract specialist must have some education in accounting, business, law, or economics. He or she must know how to get the highest-quality products for the most reasonable price. A contract specialist can earn $44,000 to $83,000 per year, depending on education and years on the job.

Intelligence Operations Specialist

Intelligence operations specialists look for possible threats to transportation facilities. This specialist must have a college education or technical experience. He or she can earn $44,000 to $102,000 a year. This depends on knowledge, experience, and years on the job.

Information Technology Specialist

Information technology specialists help to develop computer systems. They give technical support when needed. There are many types of information technology jobs. Some positions do not require a college degree if the person has the right kind of experience. The annual salary starts at $36,400 and can go up to $83,900.

In 2006, the various departments of the DHS were working on more than 250 projects to improve security at airports and land facilities, many of which directly involve the TSA. The world of airport security—including its employees—is growing.

Bomb-sniffing dogs are a crucial part of airport security. They are also used at train depots and other mass-transit sites.

Chapter 5

TSA-Trained Protectors: Bomb-Sniffing Dogs and Federal Air Marshals

Bomb-sniffing dog teams and federal air marshals are two more partners in the mission to protect the United States from terrorist attacks. The TSA's Canine Program trains dogs to find bombs and other explosives in luggage or on aircraft. They also look for explosives at mass-transit facilities. In the future, TSA dogs will be on hand at more railroad stations across the country. Seaports will use them as well.

Federal air marshals are law enforcement officers. Their job is to stop anyone who threatens travelers' safety in airports and on flights. A federal air marshal looks like all other passengers. A terrorist or hijacker should not be able to tell that a federal air marshal is on board an aircraft.

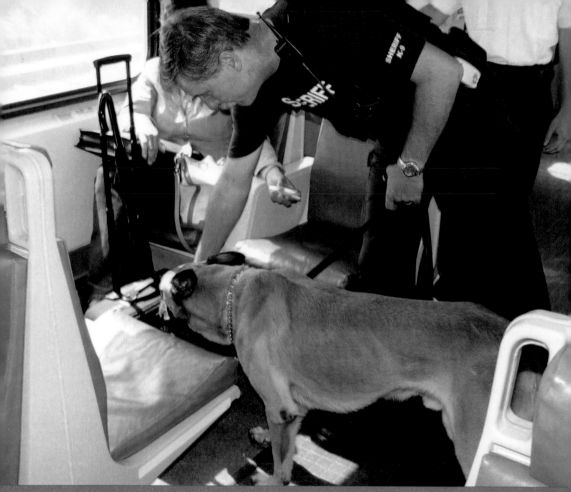
A bomb-sniffing dog checks a bag aboard a train.

Canine Coordinators

TSA canine (dog) coordinators work at airports or railroad stations with special law enforcement officers called canine handlers. The handlers do not work for the TSA. They work for the local law enforcement authorities that protect the airport. The TSA does train handlers in their work with dogs, however. Canine coordinators make sure the dogs and their handlers continue to perform well after they have been trained.

Here is an example of a typical day for a canine coordinator.[1] First the coordinator arrives for work at the airport. Then she meets with the handlers who will be on duty that day. She checks to make sure the dogs are alert and ready to work.

Often the canine coordinator will go through a review training session with handlers and their dogs. For example, she takes one dog-and-handler team to a car-rental parking lot. About twenty cars are lined up. Two or three cars have explosive devices in them. The canine coordinator watches as the handler takes the dog through the cars. She makes sure the dogs still know the best way to search through a vehicle. She may also work with another team in a warehouse. There she makes sure the dog can find explosives in shipping crates.

Later on in the day, the coordinator writes reports and sends them to the TSA headquarters. She may need to provide information about the airport's operations or any incidents that happened that day.

Sometimes there is a bomb scare in the terminal or on a plane at the gate. The airline notifies the airport command center. The passengers and all cargo are taken off the plane. The local police conduct the bomb search and report their findings to the TSA. Then they send handlers to conduct the search. The canine coordinator oversees the use of the dogs. Still, she cooperates with the police in charge and reports the incident to the TSA headquarters. She knows it is important for all of them to work together.

TSA canine coordinators train for two weeks in Oklahoma City. They learn about the TSA's needs, how to interact with handlers and dogs, and how to work with local police departments. Canine coordinators should have some education and background in criminal justice. Their salary ranges from $54,000 to $83,000 a year, depending on job location and level of experience. One TSA canine coordinator said, "I love dogs and I love the diplomacy and interacting with people. The relationship that I have with the local police works. The program works. I believe in what I am doing."[2]

The TSA Canine Program

On August 5, 2005, Southwest Airlines was making a routine flight from Dallas to Houston. A passenger found a note in a seat pocket. The note said there was a bomb on the plane. When the passenger reported this to the crew, the flight proceeded to the nearest airport in Houston.

The plane landed, and the passengers and crew were quickly evacuated. Canine officers and TSA employees immediately brought bomb-sniffing dogs onto the aircraft. No explosives were found. All the passengers and their luggage were screened once more. TSA and law enforcement people interviewed the passengers. They wanted to find out if anyone had noticed anything suspicious. The note was later found to be a prank. The man who wrote it was arrested.

This story has a happy ending, but passengers might have been delayed further if the canine force had not been there. It takes hours for a bomb squad with the best equipment to detect explosives in a one-aisle plane. Canine teams can do the same job in

History of the Canine Program

On March 9, 1972, a TWA flight was heading from New York's Kennedy Airport to Los Angeles. Shortly after takeoff the pilot received a radio message. An anonymous phone caller claimed there was a bomb on board the aircraft. The pilot immediately turned back to Kennedy Airport.

Kennedy emergency crews evacuated passengers as quickly as possible. As people streamed out of the plane, a bomb-sniffing dog named Brandy strained at her leash. She led her handler in a race against time. Brandy was trained to recognize the smell of explosives. Her nose snuffled over luggage. Buried in a bag, a hidden clock ticked down the seconds. Brandy found the bomb twelve minutes before it was set to explode.

Brandy was a pioneer. Her success helped launch the canine teams on duty at airports all over the country today. In 1972 the federal government created the Federal Aviation Administration Explosives Detection Canine Team Program. This program is now handled by the TSA. Today the program is available to airlines at most of the larger airports in the United States.[3]

about twenty-five to thirty minutes. A canine's strong sense of smell is very useful in detecting explosives. Bomb-sniffing dogs are brought into rail stations, airport terminals, and seaports whenever there is a bomb threat. Each bomb-sniffing dog works with only one handler. At Chicago's busy O'Hare Airport, for example, the Chicago Police Department is in charge of the canine handlers. The handlers work closely with TSA personnel.

Training the Dog and Handler

A person interested in joining the canine program must already be a law enforcement officer. Once officers are accepted into the program, they are trained at the TSA Explosives Detection Canine Handler Course at Lackland Air Force Base in San Antonio, Texas. The canine handler is paired with a dog such as a Labrador retriever or German shepherd. These breeds are chosen because they are gentle and have strong senses of hearing and smell. Some dogs are bred by TSA's breeding program. Others are brought from Europe. The dogs must be healthy, smart, and highly motivated. Each dog is named after a person killed on September 11, 2001.

When canine program puppies are nine weeks old, they are sent to live with a foster family in the San Antonio area. This helps the puppy get used to being around people. The family feeds and cares for the puppy according to TSA orders.

The TSA depends on volunteer families in the San Antonio, Texas, area to act as foster families to TSA puppies. The families take the puppies at age nine weeks and keep them until they are about twelve months old. The families are asked to give the puppies a friendly and caring home.

The TSA supplies food, equipment, and medical care for the puppies. For a few days each month, the pups are sent to the TSA for medical checkups. This gives the TSA a chance to do additional training as needed. The pups are later returned to the Puppy Program for their final training and evaluations. If qualified, the pups are sent for official explosive detection training at a TSA facility.

Training the Dog

TSA trainers work with canine foster families to be sure they are handling the dog correctly. The families must keep a daily journal of the dog's activities. The trainers check the journal and tell the families if they are not working properly with the dog. For example, family members must not play too much with the dog. If the dog plays too often with the kong—a toy provided by TSA trainers—he soon becomes bored and loses interest. If he loses interest in the reward as a puppy, then he will be difficult to train. This is important because, later on, the kong will be the dog's reward for finding an explosive.

If the trainer sees that the foster family is not working with the dog properly, the dog is brought back to the Air Force base. The dog may be kept in the kennel most of the day, except for a short play period each week. This will make playing with the kong a special event for him.

As the dogs get older, the trainers start to teach them explosives detection. It can take as many as fifty trials a day before the dog learns the smell of the first explosive sample. It can take that long again to find the smell of the second sample. After several days the dog learns to recognize a dozen explosives, such as dynamite and nitroglycerin. When he detects an explosive, he sits and stares at it. Then he gets his reward—the kong. The kong is now so special to him that he will work very hard to find the explosives.

Once the dog is old enough, it receives special training on how to detect explosives.

The dog is usually about fourteen weeks old when he meets his handler. The handler becomes his owner and master. The handler is usually a policeman, a Border Patrol officer, or someone in a sheriff's department. Now the TSA trainer must show the handler how to work with the dog.

Training takes about eleven weeks. TSA trainers show the officer how to work with a dog as it sniffs for explosives. Sometimes the dogs lose interest in the search. When that happens, the trainers keep the handler and the dog inside where it is quiet. The trainers teach the handler how to guide the dog and keep him focused. The handler also learns how to tell when his

> The handler and the dog take a certification test. If the dog finds fourteen out of fifteen cars containing explosives, the handler has passed the test.

dog has found an explosive. TSA trainers also show the officer how to handle explosives. As the dog and the handler work together, they become a team.

Then it is time for the certification test. The handler and the dog have to find explosives in a long row of luggage. If they are successful, they are taken to a parking lot full of old cars. Again, the TSA trainer tells the handler and the dog to search for explosives. The handler must be careful to watch the dog's movements. If the dog finds fourteen out of fifteen cars containing explosives, the handler has passed the test. If the handler senses the dog has found a car with explosives but moves on without making sure, it counts against the handler. After training, handlers must be 100-percent certain that they have found all the explosives.[4] If one device is not found due to carelessness, many lives can be lost.

The training is completed at the end of ten weeks. The handler and the dog return to the airport or the police department where the handler works. The dog lives and works with only one handler. It becomes part of the handler's family. The team goes through several hours of retraining each week. This helps the dog get used to the thousands of odors, noises, and movements in a transportation facility.

Each year the dog and handler go through several days of testing. They have to get recertified by the TSA. The agency needs to be sure the handler and the dog still have the skills to be in the program.

The Dog's Job

The handler and dog team spend part of each day at the airport. They walk through the terminals and search for anything unusual, such as an unattended piece of luggage. The dog is trained to sniff the bag for explosives. If it finds none, the handler moves on.

If an explosive device is found, the police are called and the command center is notified. Sometimes the airport receives an anonymous note or phone call that a bomb has been planted. Sometimes an officer may hear a casual remark, such as a person saying the word *bomb*.

The officer and his dog are called. All threats and remarks are taken seriously.

The number of U.S. canine handlers has increased since the bombings in London and Madrid. Canine teams now work on buses, railroads, and elevated trains in large cities. Dogs need to get used to searching for explosives on moving vehicles. This is another challenge for the dog and its handler.

Federal Air Marshals: Protection at 30,000 Feet

The hijackings of September 11, 2001, were some of the most shocking in history—but they were not the first. Hijacking goes back almost fifty years.[5] Between 1958 and 1969 there were 177 hijacking attempts on U.S. and foreign airplanes.

During the first few years, most of the attempts were on flights beginning in Cuba. There had been a revolution in Cuba, and the new government placed strict control on travel outside the country. People who wanted to leave Cuba would hijack a plane and try to force the pilot to fly to the United States. When the U.S. government banned all travel between the United States and Cuba, Cubans living in the United States hijacked flights. They demanded that the pilots fly the plane to Cuba.

In the early 1960s President John F. Kennedy established the U.S. Sky Marshal Program. He hoped this would reduce hijackings. The government put

The U.S. Sky Marshal Program was established after a rash of hijackings in the late 1950s and 1960s.

officers called marshals on commercial airliners when the airlines or the FBI requested them. A new law stated that a hijacker could get the death penalty or at least twenty years' imprisonment for the crime. Hijackings decreased for the next several years.

Then, in 1968 and 1969, hijackings increased again. Some hijackers took over the plane and demanded money. Other hijackings happened on foreign soil.

Terrorist groups took over planes and demanded the release of political prisoners.

In January 1969 the FAA created a task force to stop hijacking. The task force developed a hijacker profile. This was a set of traits, or qualities, that a hijacker might have. The profile was used to identify people who fit the profile. Airline personnel also began to use metal detectors.

In 1970 President Richard Nixon established a full-time Sky Marshal Program. These sky marshals provided armed security aboard U.S. aircraft. This helped lessen hijacking incidents in the United States up to 1985.

Then, in June 1985, a TWA flight was hijacked as the plane departed from Athens, Greece. The pilot was forced to fly to Beirut, Lebanon. In Beirut additional hijackers joined the terrorists. They demanded the release of some political prisoners who were being held in Israel. The incident lasted two weeks. One of the passengers was killed.

In 1985 President Ronald Reagan expanded the Sky Marshal Program, and it became the Federal Air Marshal Service. By 1987, four hundred air marshals were in service on U.S. flights. Over the next fourteen years, the number of marshals declined.

Federal Air Marshals—
Before and After September 11
In 2001 there were only thirty-three federal air marshals (FAMs). When President Bush created the TSA in

Until 2005, Immigration and Customs Enforcement ran the Federal Air Marshal Service. Now the TSA coordinates the activities of all federal air marshals on commercial flights.

November 2001, he ordered an increase in the number of air marshals. The Federal Air Marshal Service was transferred from the FAA to Immigration and Customs Enforcement. In October 2005 it became part of the TSA.

In a very short time the Federal Air Marshal Service received more than 200,000 FAM applications.

Air marshals receive their initial training at the Federal Law Enforcement Training Center in Artesia, New Mexico.

Applicants were screened. Those hired were trained and certified. Today FAMs are present on flights all over the world. The actual number of marshals cannot be revealed because it is protected from the public.[6]

FAMs on the Job: Quiet Professionals
FAMs must make split-second, life-and-death decisions at 30,000 feet in the sky. They must be able rely on their training to protect passengers' lives. They try to blend

in with passengers while remaining constantly aware of their surroundings.

The purpose of the Federal Air Marshal Service is to find and defeat anyone who attempts to commit hostile acts against U.S. air carriers, airports, passengers, and crews. FAMs dress and look like other passengers aboard the aircraft. Only the flight crew and security personnel know who they are. It would be impossible to place an air marshal on every U.S. flight. Their assignments are kept secret to discourage hijackings and other incidents on every flight.

FAMs carry a firearm. They can make an arrest without a warrant to protect people on board an

The Surveillance Detection System

The Federal Air Marshal Service is going one step further in combating terrorism. The service has developed the Surveillance Detection System (SDS). This is a way to share information. FAMs observe possible suspicious actions in an airport or on an aircraft. Then the marshal reports this behavior into a database to be analyzed. Other law enforcement agencies study this information for patterns of terrorism.

FAMs use SDS information and view other reports on their personal digital assistants (PDAs). This is one way FAMs can stop terrorist acts before they happen. They share all information with others in the federal law enforcement community.

aircraft. They use the least amount of force necessary in order to gain control of the situation and to ensure the safety of the aircraft, the passengers and crew, and themselves. They also help if there is an in-flight emergency, such as when a passenger has a heart attack.

A FAM needs to know several law enforcement techniques. These include surveillance, interviews, and questioning suspects. FAMs make arrests, conduct searches and seizures, and do background checks. They must know how to use wireless devices, cameras, and other equipment that must be kept classified. The marshals testify in court and carry out undercover assignments.

Calming an Unruly Passenger

On a Northwest Airlines flight from Pittsburgh to Minneapolis, the flight crew learned that a woman was annoying other passengers with loud and offensive comments. She was moved to a seat in the rear. Then she started blocking passengers from the restroom area. An air marshal tried to calm her down by taking a seat next to her. At that point, the woman threatened to kill the air marshal. She hit him and tried to choke him, but he overpowered and handcuffed her. When the flight arrived in Minneapolis, the woman was arrested and charged with assaulting a federal officer and interfering with a flight crew.[7]

Working as a FAM is a demanding job. FAMs travel for several weeks at a time, both in the United States and internationally. This means they work long and irregular hours and are on call twenty-four hours a day. They are not always able to keep in touch with their families. Time off can be limited. They spend long days alone in airports and in flight. Sometimes they travel to countries that are unsafe because of political or economic situations. Other areas may have possible health hazards such as poor sanitation and unsafe water.

What It Takes to Be a FAM

People applying to be a federal air marshal must meet several requirements:

- They must be U.S. citizens under the age of forty at the time they apply.
- They must have three years of general experience or a bachelor's degree in any professional, technical, or investigative field.
- They must have one year of experience in law enforcement, such as criminal investigation or aviation security. In place of that they can have a doctoral degree or three years of education in criminal justice, law, police science, or aviation management.
- Applicants must undergo psychological testing and meet strict fitness guidelines.

A Dangerous Dress Code

In 2004 the *Washington Times* reported that federal air marshals (FAMs) were required to follow strict dress and grooming codes. These codes could have put them in danger. These days, fewer and fewer airline passengers dress up for a flight, yet male FAMs reportedly had to wear a suit or a coat and tie. No beards were allowed. Female marshals had to wear business suits. Both men and women had to wear their hair in plain styles, and dress shoes were required. Did the code make FAMs too easy to pick out in a crowd?

The paper's criticism of the program worked. In 2005 the Federal Air Marshal Service relaxed its dress code. In the interest of anonymity, the agency keeps its exact requirements a secret.[8]

The FAM training program has two parts. The first is a seven-week officer-training program at the Federal Law Enforcement Training Center in Artesia, New Mexico. Air marshal students learn law, marksmanship, and physical fitness. They study defense tactics and emergency medical techniques. They also concentrate on law enforcement practices.

The second phase takes place at the FAMS Training Academy in Atlantic City, New Jersey. FAM trainees learn how to defend passengers against people who threaten passengers while in flight. The trainees learn to observe people's behavior and to watch for actions that could be dangerous to others.

FAMs are trained on a mock-up aircraft that looks somewhat like a movie set. The plane is filled with mannequins instead of people. Trainees work with guns and live ammunition. Training also happens in a real jet with an especially wide body. The jet is like a laboratory where FAMs study ways to overcome hijackers. They go through role-playing sessions and

> FAMS must know how to deal with a violent passenger in the cockpit or cabin of an aircraft.

use paintball-style ammunition. They must know how to deal with a violent passenger in the cockpit or cabin of an aircraft.

FAM candidates must be able to operate the latest firearms. They need excellent marksmanship skills. FAMs must be more accurate with a handgun than officers of any other law enforcement agency because they work in such a small space. They must be able to hit the terrorist or hijacker while missing the innocent people, all in a narrow space. They also learn how to handle emergencies such as terrorist hijackings on several types of aircraft, from a wide-body

Federal air marshals must train for real-life hostage situations. This trainee's face is blurred to keep his identity secret.

jet to a plane with just one aisle. They must know what they are legally allowed to do to keep travelers safe while controlling an unruly passenger. FAMs skills with firearms are retested about every three months.

Air Marshal

After graduation from the training program, FAMs are ready to begin flying missions. Marshals have no backup while in flight. They cannot call for assistance from other law enforcement personnel. They rely only on their instincts and training. FAMs can earn between $36,000 and $83,900 per year. Their salary depends on their experience, education, and level of responsibility.

A guidance counselor can provide a lot of help to students who are interested in a future with the TSA.

Chapter 6

Planning for the Future

Planning for a career in the Transportation Security Administration can start as early as high school. The TSA offers several opportunities for young people to learn about its mission and to decide which jobs interest them the most.

This is where the planning starts. Keep in mind that the TSA—and any government agency—wants to know many things about its applicants. The TSA checks applicants' backgrounds to ensure they do not have a criminal record. The TSA hiring staff is also concerned with drug use. Many people who apply for jobs have to pass a drug screening.

Since 2002, colleges across the country have begun offering degrees or courses in homeland security. Various

Government agencies (including the TSA) use a system called KSA to decide if a person is suited to a particular job. KSA stands for knowledge, skills, and ability.

Knowledge means education. Some jobs require a college education. Others, such as a TSO, require no more than a high-school education. Applicants must still know how to read, write, and speak English. Other jobs require education in a field such as engineering or law enforcement.

Skills refer to a person's talents. Some people may be good at math. Others express their thoughts well in writing and when speaking. This means they have communication skills. For higher-paying jobs, applicants need to know how to manage and supervise people. People skills—the ability to get along with various kinds of people—are required for almost all jobs in the TSA.

Abilities are different from skills. If a person has an ability, it means he or she can perform a specific task when he or she applies for a job. For example, a person may have good writing skills but may not have the ability to write a technical report. It could also mean the ability to organize one's workload, to manage specific types of people, or to operate technical and security equipment.

programs in homeland security, information security, and police service are also offered online.

Volunteer and Internship Opportunities

The TSA and the DHS help high-school and college students gain experience in the homeland security field. The agencies offer volunteer and part-time job programs that can fit into a student's class schedule. These programs are offered in airports around the country. Some jobs give academic credit for work experience, while others are paid jobs. Some are offered only for college students. Others require only that you attend high school full- or part-time.

The Student Temporary Employment Program (STEP) offers summer or part-time jobs for young people while they are students. Duties may include typing information into a computer database or filing.

The Student Career Experience Program (SCEP) gives students work experience similar to subjects they are studying at school. SCEP participants may also earn academic credit. It may even lead to a permanent job after graduation.

Both these programs can be full-time or part-time. Applicants must have a grade point average of 2.0 or higher based on a scholastic average scale of 4.0. Finally, all participants must be U.S. citizens.

The Student Volunteer Service Program (SVSP) gives students the chance to gain experience working

An intern works at the U.S. Marshals office in Dayton, Ohio.

with the TSA. It is open to high-school, college, or vocational-school students. As the name suggests, it is a volunteer program. The position is not paid, but the experience helps in planning one's future career. Grades are still important for this program. All students must have at least a 2.0 grade point average on a 4.0 scale.

The Department of Homeland Security Scholarship Program is open to students interested in science and technology. Students receive money to study subjects such as science, mathematics, computer and information, social sciences, and engineering.

Where to Go from Here

So where should you go from here? You might not be ready to make a major career decision yet, and that is fine. Most people start out thinking they are suited for one type of job but may change their minds. People change as they grow, and so do their interests and abilities.

A federal security director at one of the nation's largest airports once handled security for a football team. After September 11 he decided to use his abilities in handling security situations at the TSA. On the other hand, a current transportation security officer worked with machinery for most of his career. Then he applied to the TSA because he felt it was where he could best serve his country. Both of these men receive a tremendous amount of satisfaction from their jobs. Neither can imagine doing anything else. They enjoy the constant challenges that their jobs present each day.[1]

How the TSA Helps Employees Move Up

The TSA has created programs that help its employees set their goals in the coming years. For example, TSOs may work toward becoming a lead officer and then a supervisory officer or a training coordinator. If they want to stay in screening, they can move up to screening manager. From there they can become an assistant FSD for screening.

The TSA transportation security officers can be promoted after two years if they qualify. Eventually they can apply for other homeland security jobs. These can include areas such as technology or

customs and immigration inspection. Of course, they have to show the ability to be trained for other jobs.[2]

You might not be thinking that far ahead, but it still helps to work out a self-assessment. This is a series of questions about what type of person you are, what work environment you like best, and where you can best use your knowledge, ability, and skills. Most of all, ask yourself about your likes and dislikes. This works for any career you may be considering. These questions will help you decide what kind of TSA job is right for you:

1. What jobs require skills and knowledge that I already have?

2. Can I work independently, without people helping me?

3. Do I want daytime hours, or am I willing to work nights and weekends if necessary?

4. Do I like background noise and lots of activity, or do I prefer quiet surroundings?

5. How about changes in routine—can I handle change, or do I want to do the same thing every day?

6. Do I want to sit in one spot all day, or do I like lots of moving around?

7. Do I like working indoors or outdoors?[3]

The following quotes are from travelers who took the time to compliment TSA employees:

The experience of the 156,000 daily passengers at [Dallas/Fort Worth International] Airport has changed considerably since September 11, 2001. The unprecedented terrorist attacks on that day forced an overhaul of the nation's airport security system, bringing higher-paid government screeners, more thorough checks and a lengthy set of restrictions. "It's a very positive thing. I want to feel a little more secure when I travel," said Joanne Klausner as she waited in line before her flight to Norfolk, VA. "I can remember traveling years ago when they barely asked you for identification."[4]

—*A news story in the* Dallas Morning News

I am writing on behalf of my family to thank your officers for making our recent travel such a pleasant experience. Last month I was traveling with my parents who are both in their 70s. They had not flown since 9/11 and were concerned about the new security measures. . . . The TSA officers . . . not only dealt with my parents in a considerate, helpful manner, but their good attitudes alleviated [relieved] any further stress my parents had about flying. They were professional and friendly. . . . Thanks so much for the great officers.[5]

—*Larissa FastHorse of Santa Monica, California, writing to Esmeralda Gonzalez, Customer Support and Quality Improvement Manager, Los Angeles International Airport, October 11, 2005*

I want to recognize particularly kind and helpful assistance from a TSA employee. Fred Molliner at the Monterey [California] airport helped me considerably when I showed up to try and check in after a trade show with three checked bags. I was already at my limit for carry-ons, and would have had to pay a steep premium for the third checked bag. He observed that two of the checked boxes were small and of very similar size, so he quickly and efficiently taped them together for easy handling. I really appreciate what the TSA staff does every day. TSA staff and procedures are so clearly an improvement over the perfunctory [thoughtless] and indifferent inspections that happened before 9/11.[6]

—*A letter to Stacy Everett, Customer Support and Quality Improvement Manager, Monterey Peninsula Airport*

The TSA is constantly striving to ensure safety for travelers. Its employees work hard on developing technology, improving relations with other government agencies, and making transportation systems safer. The threat of terrorism will not go away any time soon. Perhaps it never will. However, the TSA and its thousands of employees are making every effort to see that the threat is kept as low as possible.

Chapter 1. Guarding the Skies

1. "About TSA," *TSA.gov*, n.d., <http://www.tsa.gov/public/display?theme=7> (March 28, 2006).

Chapter 2. September 11: A Wake-up Call

1. The 9/11 Commission, "The 9/11 Commission Report," *National Commission on Terrorist Attacks Upon the United States*, n.d., <http://www.9-11commission.gov/report/index.htm> (June 15, 2006).

2. "What Went Right," *Aviation Week and Space Technology*, September 9, 2005, <http://www.*tsa.gov*/public/display?content=090005198016ab8d> (March 28, 2006).

3. Byron Okada, "Screeners Kept Flights Moving," *Dallas-Fort Worth Star-Telegram*, September 12, 2005, p. B1.

4. Ibid.

5. Andrea Domaskin, "Airport Security Worker Helps in Katrina Relief," *The Forum* (South Dakota), September 26, 2005, p. 8.

6. "What Went Right."

7. George W. Bush, "President Bush Signs Aviation Security Legislation," *TSA.gov*, November 19, 2001, <http://www.tsa.gov/public/display?theme=38&content=0900051980003124> (March 28, 2006).

8. Emily Hollis, "Transportation Security Administration: Safety in Numbers," *Chief Learning Officer*, July 2003, <http://www.tsa.gov/travelers/airtravel/prohibited/permitted-prohibited-items.shtm> (July 18, 2006).

Chapter 3. How the Transportation Security Officer Makes Travel Safe

1. "Permitted and Prohibited Items List," *TSA.gov*, March 2, 2006, <http://www.tsa.gov/travelers/airtravel/prohibited/permitted-prohibited-items.shtm> (October 10, 2006).

2. "Artfully Concealed Items Confiscated by TSA Screeners," *TSA.gov*, n.d., <http://www.tsa.gov/public/display?theme=8&content=090005198004c2ca> (March 28, 2006).

3. Reuters, "Bomb Components Found at San Diego Airport," *Planenews.com*, n.d., <http://planenews.com/modules.php?name=News&file=article&sid=3987> (March 28, 2006); Michael Stetz, "Terminal shut: weapons of mass distraction," *San Diego Union-Tribune*, October 26, 2005, <http://www.signonsandiego.com/uniontrib/20051026/news_7m26scare.html> (March 28, 2006).

4. "Lead Security Officer Acts Quickly After Woman Collapses," *TSA.gov*, n.d., <http://www.tsa.gov/who_we_are/people/profiles/richard_hale.shtm> (August 14, 2006).

5. Discussions and e-mail correspondence with Lara Uselding, TSA public affairs officer, Chicago, Illinois, July 2005; August 19–23, 2005; Jan. 4–31, 2006; April 5–13, 2006.

6. "Federal Flight Deck Officer Overview," *TSA.gov*, n.d., <http://www.tsa.gov/lawenforcement/programs/ffdo.shtm> (October 10, 2006).

7. "TSA's Pledge to Travelers," *TSA.gov*, n.d., <http://www.tsa.gov/public/display?content=09000519800fd5b2> (March 28, 2006).

8. Interview with Robert Becker, lead baggage officer at O'Hare International Airport, July 26, 2005.

Chapter 4. TSA Technology: Staying Ahead of the Terrorists

1. "Initiatives Touch All Modes of Transportation," *TSA.gov*, n.d., <http://www.tsa.gov/public/display?theme=253> (March 28, 2006).

2. Interview with Walter Wall, systems analyst and requirements engineer, branch manager at the William J. Hughes Technical Center, Atlantic City, New Jersey, February 14, 2006.

3. Discussions and e-mail correspondence with Lara Uselding, TSA public affairs officer, Chicago, Illinois, July 2005; August 19–23, 2005; Jan. 4–31, 2006; April 5–13, 2006.

4. Ibid; "Registered Traveler Pilot Program," *TSA.gov*, n.d., <http://www.tsa.gov/public/display?content=09000519800b4ddd> (March 28, 2006).

5. "Hazmat Threat Assessment Program: Background Checks Now Required for Hazmat Truck Drivers," *TSA.gov*, n.d., <http://www.tsa.gov/public/display?content=0900051980114 cb1> (March 28, 2006).

6. Jo-Ann Moriarty, "Fighting Terror with Technology," *The Republican*, September 23, 2004, p. A01.

7. "PortSTEP Program Initiated," *TSA.gov*, August 18, 2005, <http://www.tsa.gov/public/display?content=090005198015c 2cd> (March 28, 2006).

8. "Transit and Rail Inspection Pilot Programs," *TSA.gov*, n.d., <http://www.tsa.gov/public/interapp/editorial/editorial_1711. xml> (March 28, 2006).

9. "Secretary Ridge Announces the Awarding of $28 Million for Operation Safe Commerce," *TSA.gov*, July 24, 2005, <http://www.tsa.gov/public/display?content=090005198003f 277> (March 28, 2006).

10. "TSA Teams Up With The American Trucking Associations To Prevent And Respond To Terrorism," *TSA.gov*, March 23, 2004, <http://www.tsa.gov/public/display?content=0900051 980093924> (March 28, 2006).

Chapter 5. TSA-Trained Protectors: Bomb-Sniffing Dogs and Federal Air Marshals

1. Interview with Kirsten Wood, TSA Canine Coordinator at O'Hare International Airport, August 3, 2005.

2. Ibid.

3. "Canine and Explosives Program: Program History and Description," *TSA.gov*, n.d., <http://www.tsa.gov/public/display?theme=32&content=090005198003466c> (March 28, 2006).

4. Laura Meckler, "How a Pup in Training as a Bomb Sniffer Learns His Stuff," *Wall Street Journal*, December 19, 2005, p. A1.

5. "Federal Air Marshal Service: FAMS Mission and History," *TSA.gov*, n.d., <http://www.tsa.gov/public/interapp/asset_summary/asset_summary_multi_image_with_table_0359.xml> (March 28, 2006).

6. Interview with Dave Adams, point of contact for the Federal Air Marshal Service, February 14, 2006.

7. U.S. Department of Justice, United States Attorney, District of Minnesota, "Press Release," *Minnesota FBI*, January 28, 2004, <http://minneapolis.fbi.gov/pressrel/2004/sunday012804.htm> (June 22, 2006).

8. Audrey Hudson, "Air marshals' secrecy ruined by dress code," *The Washington Times*, n.d., <http://www.washingtontimes.com/national/20040709-121013-3063r.htm> (March 28, 2006).

Chapter 6. Planning for the Future

1. Interview with Edith Bianchi, stakeholder liaison, O'Hare International Airport, interviewed July 12, 2005; Interview

with Michael Zunk, federal security director, O'Hare International Airport, July 14, 2005; Interview with Robert Becker, lead baggage screener, O'Hare International Airport, July 15, 2005.

2. Stephen Barr, "A Career Track for Airport Screeners," *Washington Post*, July 20, 2006, p. D04.

3. "Getting Started: A Quick Self-Assessment," *TSA.gov*, <http://www.tsa.gov/interweb/assetlibrary/CPGQuickSelf Assessment2 .doc> (March 28, 2006).

4. "What Others Are Saying About TSA," *TSA.gov*, various dates, <http://www.tsa.gov/public/display?content= 09000519800d1002> (March 28, 2006).

5. Ibid.

6. Ibid.

anonymous—Nameless; shielded from anyone knowing one's identity.

biometrics—The technique of studying a person's physical characteristics, such as fingerprints, eye structure, or voice pattern.

candidates—People who seek a job or other position, such as an elected office.

compressed—Pressed together; flattened.

contractor—A person or company that enters into an agreement with another person or company.

density—The amount of a material in a specific amount of space.

detain—To hold back or to keep from proceeding with one's plans. When travelers are detained at an airport security checkpoint, they are kept from catching their flight until it is certain they do not pose a threat.

detect—To discover; to determine that something exists.

diplomacy—Skill in handling people without causing stress or tension.

discourage—To try to prevent.

dynamite—An explosive made of various chemicals.

engineers—People who design or build machines, buildings, vehicles, electrical systems, and other things.

evacuated—Cleared out; sent away.

facility—A building that serves a particular purpose, often professional.

forbidden—Disallowed; illegal.

Global Positioning System—A fleet of communication satellites that can find the location of a point on the earth's surface.

hazardous—Threatening; an explosive or a dangerous chemical would be hazardous to people's lives.

hijack—To take control of a vehicle.

hostile—Unfriendly; involving an enemy.

instincts—Natural behaviors or thoughts that happen without a person's control.

intelligence—Information concerning an enemy or possible enemy.

iris—The colored part of the eye.

law enforcement—A group or person that is charged with making sure laws are obeyed.

liaison—A person who helps two people or organizations communicate well.

mannequin—A humanlike figure created by an artist.

manufacturers—People or companies that make products.

mass transit—A system for moving large crowds of people from one place to another, such as buses, trains, and subways.

motivated—Excited about doing something.

nitroglycerin—A heavy, oily, explosive liquid used in making dynamite.

prohibited—Forbidden; disallowed.

prosthetic devices—Man-made objects that replace body parts.

psychological testing—Procedures done to measure the health or normality of a person's mind and behavior.

rehabilitation—Recovering from or coping with an injury, disease, or disability.

replicas—Copies; models.

restricted—Limited; closed off to some people.

security checkpoints—Places in airports (or other public buildings) where baggage or carry-on bags are checked for dangerous items, weapons, or explosives.

stakeholder—A person who has a special interest in something.

standards—Guidelines or specifications that make sure something or someone is of high quality.

subdued—Brought under control.

surveillance—Close watch over someone or something.

suspicious—Questionable; not trustworthy.

swab—A piece of material, usually cotton, on the end of a stick or wire.

technology—The use of knowledge, such as how to write a computer program or to build a specialized device, to achieve a complicated task.

terrorists—People who use force or violence to try to overthrow a government or disrupt a society.

three-dimensional—Having height, width, and depth; true to life; not flat.

toxic—Poisonous.

turpentine—An oil used to clean up paint or to make it thinner.

undercover—Secret; disguised.

unique—Special; unlike anything else.

unruly—Unable to be disciplined or controlled.

warrant—An official document or commission to do something. In most cases, law enforcement personnel must have a warrant to arrest someone. However, federal air marshals can make an arrest without a warrant.

Books

Beyer, Mark. *Sky Marshals.* New York: Children's Press, 2003.

Damp, Dennis V. *The Book of U.S. Government Jobs.* La Crosse, Wis.: Brookhaven Press, 2005.

Hutton, Donald P., and Anna Mydlarz. *Guide to Homeland Security Careers.* Hauppauge, N.Y.: Barron's Educational, 2003.

Wright, John. *The U.S. Transportation Security Administration.* Broomall, Pa.: Mason Crest Publishers, 2003.

Internet Addresses

The TSA Web site
    <http://www.tsa.gov>

The Department of Homeland Security
    <http://www.dhs.gov/dhspublic/>

The Federal Aviation Administration
    <http://www.faa.gov>

A

airport security measures, 18–19, 20–21, 23, 26–27
American Trucking Association (ATA), 24, 76
Aviation and Transportation Security Act, 20, 24

B

backscatter, 64
baggage officer, 37, 42–44
baggage, screening of, 37, 42, 44
biometrics, 64, 66, 68, 70
Bush, George W., 20, 94–95

C

canine coordinator, 13, 54, 82–84
canine handler, 82–86, 88–92
Canine Program dogs, bomb-sniffing, 81, 83, 84–85, 86, 88–92
history of, 85
Puppy Program, 87
training, 86, 88–91
career planning, 109
contract specialist, 54, 78
customer support and quality improvement manager, 54, 55–56

D

dangerous goods and cargo inspector, 56–57
Department of Homeland Security (DHS), 10, 12, 18, 20–21, 24, 59–63, 69, 74, 78, 79, 107, 109
Department of Transportation, 20, 24
document scanner, 64
dogs, bomb-sniffing. *See* Canine Program.

E

engineer, 47, 51, 54, 59–63
explosives, detection of
Explosives Detection Canine Team Program, 85
explosives detection system (EDS), 27, 45–46, 51
explosives trace detection (ETD), 27, 39, 45–46, 51
improvised explosive device (IED), 37, 40

F

federal air marshal, 9–10, 12–13, 18, 34, 54, 81, 92–103
Federal Air Marshal Training Academy, 100

Federal Bureau of Investigation (FBI), 8, 12, 69, 93
Federal Flight Deck Officer program, 47
Federal Law Enforcement Training Center, 100
federal security director (FSD), 18, 24, 38, 54, 55, 56, 62, 109
firearms, 19, 44, 47, 102
forbidden objects, 30, 42, 44

H

hazardous materials, licenses for, 68–69
Hazmat Threat Assessment Program, 68–69
Highway Watch, 24, 76
hijacking, 15–16, 92–94, 101
Hurricane Katrina, 18–19

I

improvised explosive device (IED), 37, 40
information, sharing, 70, 97
information technology specialist, 54, 79
intelligence operations specialist, 54, 79

K

KSA employee selection criteria, 106

L

lead transportation security officer, 44, 53, 54, 110

M

mass transit, security measures for, 63–69, 70, 72–76

N

Nixon, Richard, 94

O

Operation Safe Commerce, 74–76

P

pilot programs, 59–60, 66–69, 70, 72–76
Pledge to Travelers, 25, 48
PortSTEP (Port Security Training Exercises Program), 25, 72–73
privacy concerns, 64
program analyst, 56
program developer, 70
puffer machines, 63–64

R

Reagan, Ronald, 94
Registered Traveler Program, 25, 66–68, 70
research and development (R&D), 59–63

Ridge, Tom, 20

S

science and technology staff
(DHS), 62
screener. *See* transportation
security officer.
screening manager, 52, 54,
110
Secure Automobile
Inspection Lanes (SAIL),
25
September 11, 2001, attacks,
10, 15–17, 21, 36, 46, 52,
70, 86, 92, 109, 112
Sky Marshal Program, 92, 94
stakeholder liaison, 56
student internships, 107, 109
Surveillance Detection
System (SDS), 97

T

terrorism, 10, 12, 47, 69, 70,
72, 91–94, 97
Transportation Security
Administration (TSA)
and Hurricane Katrina,
18–19
creation of, 10, 20–21, 24
Pledge to Travelers, 25, 48
role of, 10–12, 18
time line, 24–25
Web site, 10, 31, 49

Transportation Security
Administration (TSA),
careers in
career paths, 109
employee selection
criteria (KSA), 106
employment
opportunities, 12–13
qualifications, 23,
51–52, 99
salaries, 54
training, 23, 99–103
transportation security officer
(TSO), 12, 18–19, 21, 23,
24, 25, 27, 33, 34, 36, 38,
39–40, 42, 52–53, 54, 55,
109, 110–111
transportation security
specialist, 54, 77–78
TRIP (Transit and Rail
Inspection Pilot), 24, 74

V

volunteer opportunities, 105,
107, 109

W

weapons, concealed, 7–8, 32

X

X-ray machine, 7–8, 23, 31,
37, 39, 40, 52, 60, 64, 70